AF559921

Lost Paradise

Lost Paradise

Selected Ghazals of Muneer Niazi

Translated by

Amitabha Bagchi

JUGGERNAUT BOOKS
C-I-128, First Floor, Sangam Vihar, Near Holi Chowk,
New Delhi 110080, India

First published by Juggernaut Books in 2022

10 9 8 7 6 5 4 3 2 1

P-ISBN: 9789393986429
E-ISBN: 9789393986436

Typeset in Adobe Caslon Pro by R. Ajith Kumar, Noida

Printed at Nutech Print Services - India

For Ratika

once I caught a glimpse of a captivating face
my eyes have never seen another sight like that again

Contents

Contents

Contents

Contents

Contents

Contents

Muneer Niazi: A Biographical Sketch[1]

Muneer Niazi was born in 1922 in Khanpur, a village located a few kilometres from Hoshiarpur. His mother was a Mohmand Pathan and his father a Niazi Pathan whose family traced its origin to Ghazni in Afghanistan.

for a hundred generations my ancestors have been mercenaries
I achieved honour by way of poetry

Muneer's father was an irrigation engineer who was trained at the Roorkee College of Engineering. When Muneer was just a year old, his father passed away when a large branch of a tree fell on him on a stormy day while he was at work. One of his father's brothers married Muneer's mother and became Muneer's stepfather. Despite the tragedy, Muneer had a very happy childhood in Khanpur, especially as his mother's family also lived there. Being the only boy in his mother's household, he was treated like a prince and was a great favourite of his maternal great-grandmother. He ate well, rode horses, kept pet dogs, and participated enthusiastically in all sports activities. But there was also a contemplative streak in him. He says:[2]

> *My village was very beautiful but less inhabited. I would sit by the canal and listen to the koel sing, watch the doves, count the birds while other children my age ran around.*

His time in the idyllic surroundings of Khanpur had a lasting impact on him. He kept it alive within and revisited it often in his poetry. This may also have had to do with the fact that he left Khanpur fairly early, moving to Montgomery (now Sahiwal in Pakistan) where some of his paternal uncles had established a successful transportation business.

He matriculated in 1940 while living in Montgomery. It is said that he didn't get along with his stepfather and was considered to be somewhat rebellious. So, although Muneer's intention was to study further, one of his uncles, who was an army officer, decided that the boy needed to be disciplined, and so made him enlist in the British Indian navy as a sailor. However, the navy experience did not suit Muneer. The only way he benefited from it was that his posting in Bombay brought him in touch with a literary set and gave him access to the works of the poet Meeraji (Mohammad Sanaullah Dar) and Saadat Hasan Manto, who were active literary figures in the city. Encouraged by his mother – whose primary worry was that if Muneer was martyred while in service of the British, he wouldn't get what a martyr is due in the next world – he planned to desert the navy. His first attempt, however, ended in failure. He was caught and brought back and severely punished. Eventually, he was stationed on a ship that was to sail to Singapore where the Japanese Navy was causing trouble for the British. Shortly before the ship's departure, he jumped off the deck into the open water where the ship was anchored and, despite wearing heavy naval boots, swam all the way to shore. Apocrypha further suggests that this ship was sunk by the Japanese on its way to Singapore and not a single person survived. Be that as it may, Muneer escaped being caught and eventually made his way back to Montgomery. His family realized that he was determined to leave the navy and, instead of forcing him to go back, sent him to the princely state of Bahawalpur where he would be safe from the British Military Police.

Though Muneer began his higher studies in Bahawalpur, he was more interested in playing hockey and other sports. Partly out of restlessness and partly to avoid facing academic disaster, he transferred from one college to another, moving from Bahawalpur to Lahore to Jammu to Srinagar and eventually to Jalandhar; he did not stay long in any of these places. Along the way, especially in Srinagar, he met professors who encouraged him and helped nurture the love of literature that his literate mother had instilled in him at an early age.

In Jalandhar, Muneer's studies were cut short by something altogether more horrific than the prospect of academic failure. The year 1947 came. Some of the worst communal rioting occurred in Punjab and Muneer fled home to the relative safety of Montgomery. But within days of Pakistan being formed, a massive tragedy befell his family. Two of his uncles were gunned down by the Dogra regiment for violating curfew. They had been carrying curfew passes and had ventured out at the request of the administration to get bus drivers to carry refugees to their destination. Even a wealthy and influential family like the Niazis, settled on what would later be the Pakistani side of the border for years before Partition, lost two of their precious sons. Muneer went wild with grief and burned with hatred towards Hindus and Sikhs for a long time after this incident.

In the aftermath of the killing of the two Niazi brothers, the administration tried to compensate by allotting a number of properties belonging to fleeing Sikhs to various members of the family. This led to bitter squabbling among family members and ingrained in Muneer a lifelong hatred for human avarice. Whatever share he received of the family's wealth, he ploughed into two projects: the weekly literary newsletter *Saat Rang*, which he co-edited with his friend and literary mentor Majeed Amjad, and a publishing house called Arzang. *Saat Rang* became a renowned literary periodical. Manto was also associated with it. The publishing house Arzang had a bookshop that stocked 'everything from Oscar Wilde to Meer's complete works' according to Muneer, but specialized in Russian literature based on Marxist theory, reflecting Muneer's interest in Karl Marx's writings. Muneer would later become a strong critic of the political poetry of the famous communist poet Faiz Ahmad Faiz and others like him, but in 1949 he represented Montgomery at the left-leaning All-Pakistan Progressive Writers Conference in Lahore. In 1951, he briefly associated with the short-lived left-wing Azad Pakistan Party.

In 1953, Muneer relocated to Lahore as he wanted to run *Saat Rang* from there. But he ran out of money after selling his share. However, it is also speculated that he had been cheated out of his share of the family property by his stepbrothers and, thus, the periodical could never be restarted. Instead, Muneer began writing lyrics for film songs. His unique poetic style ensured that he was soon in great demand. But, unlike most lyricists working in South

Asian films, he refused to write situation-based songs, and instead insisted that situations be tailored as per the songs. He also sold geets or songs and ghazals to periodicals and even worked at the film periodical *Screen Light* for a few years. Despite his rising fame, he always found himself in desperate financial conditions during these years, often not even having a place to sleep at night.

It was at the end of this decade, in 1959, that Muneer published his first volume of poems, *Tez Hava aur Tanha Phool* (Strong Winds and a Solitary Flower), which remains a landmark in the history of modern Urdu poetry. Over the years he published almost thirty volumes of poetry among other writings. Some of his notable collections in Urdu are *Jungle mein Dhanak* (Rainbow in the Forest), *Mah-e-Muneer* (The Brilliant Moon), *Dushmanon ke Darmiyan Shaam* (An Evening Spent with Enemies), *Aaghaz-e-Zamistan mein Dobaara* (A Return to the Beginning of Winter), *Pehli Baat hi Aakhiri Thi* (The First Thing Said Was the Last), *Syah Shab ka Samandar* (The Dark Night's Ocean) and *Chhe Rangin Darwaze* (Six Colourful Doors). He published three major collections in Punjabi and is acclaimed as a major figure in modern Punjabi poetry.

It was sometime during his early years in Lahore that Muneer married Sughra Khanam. Sughra was a widow and a relative from Muneer's mother's side. She had been diagnosed as being infertile and when Muneer decided to marry her, his mother fell into despair, leading to a long-strained relationship with her son. Sughra's death in the 1980s devastated Muneer. He was later convinced by his friends to remarry and subsequently he married Naheed Begum, who was several years his junior. Muneer never had children.

Muneer's fame hit a high note when the film *Shaheed* was released in 1962. One of the songs from this film that he had penned, 'Us Bewafa ka Shehr Hai', sung by Naseem Bano, became a major hit. Nonetheless, his professional situation remained fluid. He worked at a newspaper but had to quit because he lacked the discipline a regular job required. Over the years, he established more than one publishing house and was lauded for the quality and production of his books. Inevitably these ventures failed because he did not have the business acumen for them. In one instance he paid the writer N. M. Rashid his entire royalty before the book was even published. On being questioned by his wife, he is reported to have said, 'Earlier it was up to others to do justice or be unjust. Now it is in my hands, so I did justice.' As one of his acquaintances commented, 'He did everything in great style. The only thing he wasn't skilled at was getting by in life.'

In his later years, Muneer was recognized not just by audiences of Urdu mushairas around the world but also by the Pakistan federal government and the provincial government of Punjab that supported him financially. In 1992, he received the Pride of Performance Award – the highest literary award bestowed by the state of Pakistan. In 2005, he was awarded the Sitara-i-Imtiaz, one of Pakistan's highest civilian honours. Muneer Niazi passed away in December 2006. He left behind a wife and a legacy that has only strengthened with the passage of time.

Foreword

'Migration's Fruit'

[*A translation of Intizar Husain's essay in Urdu entitled* 'Hijrat ka Samar'][3]

Actually, I and Muneer Niazi were expelled from Paradise at the same time. These are the terms on which we have recognized each other. We run into each other here and there. Muneer Niazi starts telling me how dense the thicket of mango trees in his village was. I start talking about the way the evening fell in my village and what the peacock's cry sounded like. Muneer always tells and hears these tales as if he is telling them for the first time and hearing them for the first time. He tells his tales with a kind of melancholy and hears mine with a sense of astonishment. We carry our lost Paradise in our thoughts wherever we go. It should have been the case for others as well, but it seems everyone has made some kind of compromise or the other, or their retentive faculties have eroded. But for Muneer and I our memory has become our enemy. Memory had tormented Eve as well. She kept thinking of Paradise for years after she had been expelled from it. She would remember Paradise and weep. The tears from her eyes in memory of Paradise fell on earth and a mehndi tree grew from them. In *Qisas Al-Anbi*[4] it is written that all the mehndi trees on the face of the earth are the fruit of Eve's tears.

I like mehndi trees and Muneer's poetry. This may be because my tears are also mingled in them. When Muneer calls out to Khanpur then my heart too wants to call out to a village. When he mentions his gardens and his jungles, I leave him in his world and travel away to my own jungles. Though the jungle in my village was not very thick, my memory has made it thick. When I read Muneer Niazi's poetry, it feels like that jungle has become even thicker and spread wider. So now my jungle is thicker and more widespread, but that's not the end of it. It feels like there is some other jungle beyond that jungle. Walking in my jungle I have suddenly entered a completely different jungle, a bigger and more frightening jungle. I am afraid. It is like I am breathing in ancient times. It may be that ancient times are, indeed, to be found in our childhood.

Or is it that Muneer Niazi has made some kind of strange path with his couplets, a path that starts from Khanpur and passes through my village on the way to ancient times? So now it so happens that when I read Muneer's couplets, I travel, via my childhood, to ancient times. The fears and misgivings of childhood merge into the fears and misgivings of the man of ancient times.

> if someone calls you from behind in the jungles, Muneer
> don't ever turn around, don't turn around to see

But I think that Muneer himself has turned around and seen.

In the passage from ancient times to today, fears and misgivings have become a part of man's makeup. From the outside we appear fearless, but inside we are full of fear. Earlier we didn't turn to see, now we are scared to look within. Does some jungle lie within ourselves as well? Actually, earlier the jungle used to be outside of us, but now it is within. We came out of the jungle and built big cities and surrounded ourselves with walls, but, unknown to us, the jungle entered into us and sat hidden behind seven veils. And now it is sleeping inside us. Muneer Niazi is that person within whom the jungle has awoken and is stirring. Because, after all, he has turned and seen. While reading his poetry we feel as if we are walking in the jungle and descending into the netherworld. Strange images emerge:

> buried underground the terror of cries that are voiceless
> in a hidden dungeon something like lightning flashes
>
> will you make me ill or
> will you become the fear of the unknown
> will you stay forever in some deep layer
> like some fear in the darkness

Then strange images come to my mind too. I descend into my own netherworld. Stories from different times, tales forgotten and scattered, come back to me, like shiny, glinting pots of gold buried in the ground. Raja Basath. The golden domes of Raja Basath's palace that would shine in the darkness of the earth. My grandmother told me many stories of how these pots would travel under the ground and call out, and what would happen to the person who heard one of these calls. Her words appeared to contain a desire to hear those calls. But she used to be scared as well; what if she herself heard that call on a dark and lonely night? Snakes guard those pots. My grandmother told me that the snakes have a king. She called him Raja Basath. In the writings of the Hindu pantheon, his name is given as Raja Basuka. His palace is made of gold and shines in the darkness of the netherworld. My grandmother rarely took the snake's name. She would mention him through hints and gestures. Muneer Niazi is also scared of taking his name, but he mentions him a lot. So much fear and such attraction! But why?

Fear of the unknown and such an attraction to the unknown! This state of fear and attraction in Muneer Niazi's poetry makes one feel like Adam and Eve have just left Paradise and come to earth. The earth scares them and yet pulls them towards it. The netherworld is a mystery and the open expanse is also a mystery. The atmosphere of mystery is generated by one thing in one place and another thing in another place, and the stories of the Hindu pantheon and old fables get continuously entangled in the couplets.

the threat to this journey from its start, is it that calamity
or is it just the breeze, open the door and see

the desert of death may lie that way, beyond that point
don't go
if you want to turn back you find there is no road

For Muneer, this earth with its netherworld and its expanse is an experience of terror and wonder. But then the same question arises: Why? Does this also have to do with the story of expulsion from Paradise? Is this the fruit of migration? These mehndi trees didn't just grow on their own. Ancient man's experience is buried within you and me and within stories of the pantheon and old fables. Something must have happened, after all, for them to have come to life again with a new significance.

The clan of those who have written of the experience of migration must be separated from the other clans of Urdu literature. This experience took different forms in the writing of different writers. In Muneer Niazi, the experience has given rise to a form that creates a map of something like a new pantheon. As for the other new poetry, that can be done sitting in the teahouse without reference to any experience.

Translator's Note

There is a place where words tremble when brought face to face with their meanings. There is a world that was created by the sound of a single voice crying out. There are towns that seem to stand firm on land but actually float on water. These towns are less inhabited. Maybe they were inhabited once, maybe they were devastated by a cold wind that blew one day. Maybe one day you might fall asleep in your grief and when you wake up you are in a strange city with a seven-coloured garland lying next to you.

> in the light of the idols
> the flags of grief are drooping
>
> this is the truth, Muneer
> you are dreaming

There are things about history and geography that we all know. For example, we know that the subcontinent underwent a gory Partition. We know that this led to an irrecoverable loss for a large number of people. Muneer Niazi told the writer Mohammad Salim-ur-Rehman the following story: Every year during the monsoon Khanpur would get flooded and the entire family would move to nearby Kamalpur that remained dry and stayed there for a few weeks. After Partition when Muneer's family moved to Montgomery (now Sahiwal in Pakistan), his maternal great-grandmother, who hadn't fully understood what had happened, would often tell the younger girls of the family, 'You seem to have become too fond of Kamalpur. Don't you think it's time we went back to Khanpur?' But to go searching for the Partition, with a capital P, in Muneer Niazi's poetry is as fruitful an exercise as it is futile.

There is a couplet of Muneer's that most people in Pakistan have heard and will agree captures the tragedy of their nation:

> Muneer, has some evil spirit cast a shadow on this
> country?
> we thrash around, frantic, but travel very slowly

To seek out the tragedies of the modern nation of Pakistan, or India or Bangladesh for that matter, in this oeuvre is possible but beside the point. This is poetry meant for only one thing: to be read. Let's amend that.

This is poetry meant for two things: to be read to yourself or to be read aloud. There is no point of view in this poetry, only a point, a shifting evolving point, from which the world is viewed, or rather many worlds are viewed, many-coloured, beautiful, poisonous worlds in which the unfamiliar appears familiar and the familiar appears unfamiliar.

As we journey through the worlds of Muneer Niazi, we realize that the distinctive enchantment of these worlds is created by the poet's choice of words. We read Muneer Niazi because of his diction, his choice of words, and the way that his words come together to create the most singular image. His friend Manzur Ejaz observed, 'Muneer's diction is unique, it is unlike the diction of classical Urdu. It is a thing in itself. And no one has been able to copy it since.'

But the volume in your hands is not a volume of Urdu poetry. It may have had its genesis in one and been produced through a process of translation, but at the end of the process it stands as a volume of English poetry. Muneer may have given Urdu a new idiom. But one may ask: What does this have to do with us, the English speakers? Or, to put out a different but related question: Why translate Muneer Niazi in the first place?

Typically, translation is done in order to make works available in another language, and there is an argument to be made for the fact that, unlike Ghalib or Faiz, Muneer's work is not known to a large number of English speakers. This statement needs to be qualified. When an English language publisher in Pakistan was shown this manuscript, she declined to publish it. Her reason was that even English speakers in Pakistan know Muneer's poetry well in Urdu. So, to be precise, it can be said that Muneer's work is not known to English speakers in India, apart from the occasional social media posting of his famous nazm '*Hamesha dair kar deta hoon main*'. This naturally suggests that the purpose of translating this work was to introduce Muneer Niazi to English speakers in India not conversant in Urdu. However, this was not the main purpose of taking on this work.

I am a novelist, not a poet. But I have always felt that novelists must read poetry because it is in poetry that the outermost limits of a language can be reached and then redrawn. Those of us who work habitually in prose and wish to write a better kind of prose, have to take recourse to poetry to find out how to do what has not been done before. Poets are the ones who mine for diamonds. We prose writers take what we find, polish it a little, then set it in a well-crafted piece of jewellery and present it to our audience.

This metaphor had been with me in previous works as well but between 2014 and 2017 I wrote a novel in which I took it to the extreme. In this work, *Half the Night Is Gone*, every single passage was built around a piece of poetry. And when I say 'built around', I mean that there was a certain emotional weight I associated with a particular piece of poetry by repeating it for days and weeks to myself, sometimes for years, and that the writing of that passage was meant to be a kind of catharsis, a laying down of that weight on to the page. I successfully laid down most of what I had been carrying when I wrote that book, but a year or two after I had finished writing, Muneer Niazi was still on my mind. I began to dig deeper. It soon became clear that I was not done with his poetry. I wanted more. It felt like simply reading these ghazals had not been enough. I needed to inhabit them even more closely, to live with them for some more time before I let them go. But I had no novel project open, none on the horizon. A close friend whose literary opinions I value greatly suggested that I translate the ghazals in English. And then it struck me that in writing *Half the Night Is Gone* I had already somehow assumed that, if the writer approaches it with due humility and an open mind, the idiom of one language can be used as a guide to create an idiom in another. So, to just say it out loud: I began this translation with the conviction that Muneer's unique idiom can help create a different idiom in English. Whether as a translator I have succeeded is for you to judge.

Finally, a disclaimer. This is neither a scholarly translation nor is it comprehensive. I have translated as many ghazals as I could find, about 120 of them. My assumption is that there are probably a few that I have not been able to track down. Muneer is known for his geets and famous nazms but I haven't translated any of them. There is no good excuse for this omission, except to confess that I wasn't able to escape from the ghazal's rhythms that had entrapped me.

The reader interested in looking at the original Urdu versions of these ghazals will find three-fourths of them on Rekhta's website where they are available in the Roman, Devanagari and Nastaliq scripts. Many of the other ghazals are available in Nastaliq in the scanned versions of some of Muneer Niazi's collections that Rekhta has made available. My own source for most of the ghazals was *Intekhab-e-Kulliyaat-e-Muneer Niazi* (Farid Book Depot, Delhi, 2004) edited by Professor Farooq Argali. The ghazals appear in Nastaliq in this volume. Intizar Husain's piece is also taken from the same book.

Amitabha Bagchi
24 August 2022

Lost Paradise

Selected Ghazals of Muneer Niazi

she passed by me on her way to someone else's home

she passed by me on her way to someone else's home
trailing through the air, the scent of silken clothes

once I caught a glimpse of a captivating face
my eyes have never seen another sight like that again

heavy darkness wailed through the streets of the town
terror struck my heart when dark clouds came swirling round

a lovely pair of waiting eyes watched for him at home
who knows which desert's sun burnt that traveller to his bones

the light that came before dawn, Muneer, was filled with so
much pain
it filled my heart with sorrow, the whistle of a passing train

when the colours of spring settled on the garden then I saw

when the colours of spring settled on the garden then I saw
when the bitterness in my heart relented then I saw

I used to look at the expanse of the midnight sky
when that garden came down to earth then I saw

outside that lane, everything the eye could see had changed
when the shadows lifted from my lover's street then I saw

that face looked like something else in the drunken night
when sobriety dawned with the morning then I saw

there was another river, Muneer, looming ahead of me
I had somehow crossed one river when I saw

this girl who is standing on the balcony today

this girl who is standing on the balcony today
she is a cloud in flight or flowers in a bouquet

demurely she unfastens the buttons of her dress
a fragrance is about to fill the night's darkness

the light from a red dress fills up my gaze
a face is embedded like a jewel in my heart

my desires, like buds, once flowered over there
that window has been desolate for many, many days

the call of the peacock fills the dark with light
a hundred beautiful songs, the monsoon pours down tonight

strong drink should be drunk now that evening has come

strong drink should be drunk now that evening has come
it has been quite a while, I should now soothe my hurt

where will this beautiful garden be once you are dead?
no matter how deep the wounds, keep drawing your breath

he is wandering through the garden, deep in reverie
quietly go, snatch that rose, bring it back to me

clouds in the sky and a fragrance rising from the flower-
covered land
my beautiful one in my lap, and a bottle by my hand

fetes of red lips, Muneer, have taken over the streets
to spot them in the darkness you need an eye that can see

I was not soothed by the breeze that blew in the springtime of my grief

I was not soothed by the breeze that blew in the springtime
of my grief
and nor was that charming one to be seen on her balcony

I have suffered in separation all through this life
although I could have had you without any strife

walking down the way I saw a forgotten face
when I called out to her, I couldn't recall her name

Muneer, you kept kicking up dust in grief's wilderness
although there wasn't a single thing you wanted and didn't get

he made my entire life amount to nothing

he made my entire life amount to nothing
it was my life but he did the living

I was very weak when I first migrated to this country
and he made me weaker, even weaker in this country

deliberately he became my guide just to lead me astray
I wandered off the straight road because he led me away

I vouched for him and so he was accepted in this town
and from this town he then ensured I was hounded out

Muneer, he devastated this town, he laid it all to waste
and, do you know, he committed this cruelty in my name

I am walking down a path that doesn't lead to any goal

I am walking down a path that doesn't lead to any goal
I am hankering after things that I can never own

the weeping desert of Najd is full of lovers gone insane
every shape looks like a camel but no camel is to be seen[5]

a strange suspicion seizes hold of the beauty that hides its face
as if it has everything but is not worthy of a gaze

an open door of knowledge he stands before today
and I say to him: beware! great terror lies that way

what I want, Muneer, at the end of my days
is a different life that doesn't try me this way

my lover didn't allow me to go along that way

my lover didn't allow me to go along that way
that other home of hers remained a forbidden place

I asked my times for some time to show them that I care
my times had no time to give, my time just went away

which way does that fragrance go, which garden lies that way?
in my travels I asked the breeze, it knew but didn't say

selfishness forbade me from wasting effort for no gain
when I stood in front of that idol, it didn't let me speak
my name

to feel my powers decline, Muneer, to know I'm on the wane
I would need more talent than I have, than the Almighty gave

a stream of tears flowing fast, and me, my friends

a stream of tears flowing fast, and me, my friends
this town where infidelity lives, and me, my friends

these unfamiliar places and thoughts of those who are gone
the poison of unending loneliness, and me, my friends

it brings with it the smell of seasons that have passed
the ferocity of monsoon time, and me, my friends

wandering like a gust of wind from one town to the next
a rolling wave of waywardness, and me, my friends

a painful breeze started at the sorrowing evening's end
the last of the watches of the night, and me, my friends

festivities have turned to dust, the dust gets in my eyes
this world that advises caution to men, and me, my friends

it was a speeding arrow, it passed straight through me

it was a speeding arrow, it passed straight through me
the train let out a scream, it resounded through the trees

the town lay asleep like a snake at rest
I looked at it, transfixed, and then the moon set

their bodies burnt with a strange heat, the heat of those who crave
in the company of those beautiful women, my blood burnt away

the evening stood drenched in poisonous shades
and then in just a moment, everything had changed

Muneer, when I saw her after an age today
my heart quickened for a moment then steadied up again

all words sound alike, all sights look the same

all words sound alike, all sights look the same
all days are similar, all nights are the same

inconclusive, fruitless, war and conflict, profit and loss
all victories alike, all losses are the same

every meeting has one purpose, selling and buying, give and take
everyone fears the same thing; every ambush is the same

the fidelity of bygone times has disappeared without a trace
every clan behaves the same way, all castes are the same

similar incarcerations appear in each town's dreams
their funerals are all alike, celebrations all the same

if you're buried underground what is the value of being?
no difference between pebble and pearl, all metals are the same

Muneer, free yourself now from this strange monotony
all antidotes are similar, every poison is the same

I made a decision mindlessly, there was no reason why

I made a decision mindlessly, there was no reason why
I let my heart's desires spill beyond the boundary line

we would never be able to honour it, that we both knew
but she made a promise and I made one too

I spent freely on myself the hate my enemy had for me
and made myself into half the man I once used to be

I set down a glass of water against the colours of evening time
I made the clear liquid rival the colour of wine

was it the fear of travel or the enchantment of this ancient home?
which of these did I use to brick up the exit door?

I am turning into one of those kinds of people, Muneer,
who disallow themselves the goblet and its wine, and beauty

when I see this mortal world, it fills my heart with dread

when I see this mortal world, it fills my heart with dread
even the sight of water reminds me of death

the evening breeze enters the city of corpses through its gate
this place is weighing me down, I don't know what to say

the finish line trembles with a longing that is deep
words begin to tremble as they find out what they mean

the dust on the floor is suffering from heartbreak
it sees the home's things eager to move to a newer place

when the curtain rose, it took with it all my certainty
I'm rattled by the sight of the one who looks just like me

the villages that crossed the line, let me tell you of their state

the villages that crossed the line, let me tell you of their state
let's talk of those disciples that died along the way

remember those days when life was lived here
in these streets that later filled with ash and blood and terror

battered by strong gusts, those balconies, those doors
what a town it was, and what a wind that turned it cold

they never ever opened, what unyielding doors they were
what kinds of prayers were prayed and never answered here

abandoned ruined domes, Muneer, you're wandering in
    this place
tell me, whatever happened to your healthy, sparkling face?

you wander restless, you're anxious all the time

you wander restless, you're anxious all the time
you crackle and burn like a fire all the time

your ruby lips spill their fragrance when you walk
a garden you fill with perfume all the time

that beauty has this way, whenever love appears
it hides in its veil, acts coy every time

you make evening fall with your magical kohl
something like the moon shines in your eyes all the time

Muneer, it's a habit that you've formed for yourself
no matter which town you live, you're bored all the time

its breeze brought me back to life, this desert rain

its breeze brought me back to life, this desert rain
its fragrance was enough to make me feel new again

her being gave birth to a sense of happiness
like a garden come to bloom in a barren place

the winds of love have caused beautiful women great distress
in such times even beauty turns into pain

they're besieged somewhere up the road, the truths of our age
the ones we have been waiting to hear for so many days

Muneer, my sorrow eases when I bare my heart to her
sorrowing for whom has brought my heart to this state

one town I erase from memory, another I invent

one town I erase from memory, another I invent
in one place I create silence, in another settlements

I have to journey on my own, travelling through the night
then who do I wait for, wasting precious time?

there is some ancient name in it, this storm that blows and rains
how do I bring that forgotten name back to mind again?

I go to the garden to listen to the wind whistling through
    the trees
from the domes of ruined palaces, I see the lightning and
    feel the breeze

the morning colours the courtyard's walls, Muneer, is this
    the time to write?
or should I make the world in my words when evening turns
    to night?

the one I was thinking of came to me in thought

the one I was thinking of came to me in thought
I found within the question the answer that I sought

when he went, he went away for many, many years
when I met him again, I met him in tears

all I learned of life I learned from those who've passed away
the life of a bygone time lives in the ideals of today

after every difficult time there is another time
I knew the power of thought when it began to decline

Muneer, I saw the one whose beauty colours these new
    shoots green
in the most difficult moments of an ancient dream

I see tired people walk by, helpless and slow

I see tired people walk by, helpless and slow
it's a performance I watch from my window

if I am sad, I seek out old friends
I go and watch them sitting in silence

it tries to hide the heat in its heart but it shows
I can see the specks of colour on the face of the rose

I am standing in the courtyard of an empty fort
I can see what lies here buried in the dirt

Muneer, when I want to know the meaning of death
I go to a high place and look over the edge

like a silhouette imprisoned in a sky of blue

like a silhouette imprisoned in a sky of blue
earth and water are in awe of the brilliant moon

the forest seems to edge away from its beauty of green
it feels like the season of separation around the saint's tree

the sprawl, on a winter morning, of the city of the mean
like the face of a beggar waking from a fearful dream

in my courtyard lies a lifeless prayer for a wakefulness of mind
my desires multiply endlessly because they see the boundary line

existence is a wound only healed by that final cry
for which I wait patiently, the only thing I desire

the spell death casts, Muneer, is like the mirror's spell
all the lure of every thing comes from its likeness

leaving water and land behind, I pass by mountain and city

leaving water and land behind, I pass by mountain and city
I watch the drama being played out in front of me

sentience evaporates in the heat at this speed
I see and I forget, I forget what I see

clouds and a harassed sun up above in the sky
I am running through a desert of futility

locked in this house like a man in adversity
I endure the door and walls that stand firm around me

my poetry has moistened that cruel stony eye
and in that tearful eye I grow like a dream

Muneer, there are some desires that I walk towards
there are some sorrows in my heart I drag along with me

no escape from the dream of a rose for a man

no escape from the dream of a rose for a man
a garden, a breeze, always follows a man

he has seen these streets, these houses and people before
no matter which city he wanders, a man

I have seen such places that I am still terrorized
I have seen those faces that can scare a man

no wishes, no pearls, in the sea of now and then
will he find if he plumbs its deepest depths, a man

Muneer, with the veil of colour and fragrance on his eyes
how easily he passes the journey's stages, a man

burn this stone-hearted city to the ground

burn this stone-hearted city to the ground
then scatter its ash where it can't be found

it offers no shelter to us, no space
visit destruction upon this place

tyranny here has crossed all lines
we must punish this world for all its crimes

a thunderous sound inside every house
go to people's homes and strike fear in their hearts

Muneer, long enough you've been lost in yourself
make a little effort, let the world know you're there

go and tell time to move slowly

go and tell time to move slowly
who came to mind? my eyes grow dry of tears

why is autumn's kingdom quiet so?
a breeze should blow, or a gust of sorrow

from all sides time like an anklet sounds
when the dancing world puts its foot on the ground

come quickly, seasons of the future, why wait?
time is passing by, I'm on my way

every bubble is a palace but no one cares for its dome
the brook just flows on and on and on

from the deserted dark forests come the strains

from the deserted dark forests come the strains
the peacock drenched in colour sings songs of the rain

as evening falls their restlessness grows
the women fill with fear as the wind picks up force

the promise of divine union under night's desolate dome
in the magical sounds of the sentry's calls

draw your veil if you must, if you will, look away
he has stolen your heart, you will face him one day

if I leave this country, Muneer, where do I run?
my heart is tied to it by that exquisite thread of love

please go back home, it weeps and it pleads

please go back home, it weeps and it pleads
wherever I may go my shadow follows me

go and see him too, we are in the same state, him and I
endure your sorrow silently too long and you will die

it's not as if she doesn't love me, it just happens so
she talks freely with strangers, with me she acts demure

Muneer, with so many friends in this town, still feels alone
he puts his sorrow in his pipe and proceeds to get stoned

I drank and got so drunk that I didn't really know

I drank and got so drunk that I didn't really know
if it was that heavenly beauty or just her shadow

when I saw her yesterday, the sight was hard to see
the sorrow of our parting has broken her just like it's
    broken me

I do not know which people wept and which ones did not weep
at that time, I was miles away from my country

when the night of separation came, my heart began to sink
I am strong enough to bear it, that's what I used to think

was it a face, or was it the call of a buried memory?
were they her eyes, my friends, or was it a luminous stream?

a strong scent filled the air when the moon came out, Muneer
there was someone else in the garden apart from me

your marks remain, sorrow's rain could not wash them clean

your marks remain, sorrow's rain could not wash them clean
I did not lose you, it was you who lost me

the intoxication of sleep was still visible in his eyes
it looked like he hadn't slept till very late at night

walls and closed doors on every side, with eyes that stare at me
but my pain remains unspoken, there are no lips to speak

his tribesmen pay the price although Adam broke the law
all my life I have to reap this crop I did not sow

I too have known, Muneer, a man of that type
sadness turned him into stone, but he never cried

what is this strange forest you have wandered into, O antelopes?

what is this strange forest you have wandered into, O antelopes?
does it ever come to you, the thought of your forgotten home?

I cry tears of blood for an unknown face I had seen once then
in my mind's eye, night and day, I see that ruby from Yemen

the air in my lover's quarters is redolent of perfume
oh, her accoutrements, that body made of sandalwood

silence fills the settlements now that night has fallen
but it won't let me sleep, my heart's discontent

is it that angelic one's face, Muneer, flushed, all aflame?
or is it a garden of roses lit up by the moon's rays?

my heart burnt with sorrow but it kept singing its song

my heart burnt with sorrow but it kept singing its song
as long as life accompanied me, this talent came along

the night before the journey, there were stars and a breeze
and some kind of shadow that lingered on the balcony

the wind carried my voice a very long way
but the one I was calling out to remained unaware

what fun this life has been, slipping by in thoughts of you
this separation has been magical and very useful too

along with the sky above, terror hovered over me
is there someone here, or isn't there? my heart was full of fear

Muneer, that last look of his was filled with a strange pain
the sorrow of his going stayed with me all my days

in the sorrow of your leaving I faced no ignominy

in the sorrow of your leaving I faced no ignominy
I went completely quiet, I put up no show to see

it's that kind of journey where no one comes along
it's that kind of road on which you haven't ever been

it's been a little difficult to stay in this place
despite being here for years it feels foreign to me

whether the king was to blame or the people of this town
whatever happened here, it was an atrocity

Muneer, I wanted to meet her again some day
that was what I wanted but it was not to be

chain myself to sorrow, I am not like that

chain myself to sorrow, I am not like that
completely shut the world out, I am not like that

every day I am pulled from different sides by different thoughts
to let those thoughts rend me in two, I am not like that

many questions in my heart and that unanswering door
but to leave that door and go, I am not like that

the rigours of this journey have worn me out, Muneer
turn around and go back home, I am not like that

prisoner of desire, captive of fate, is it you or is it me?

prisoner of desire, captive of fate, is it you or is it me?
slave to the rising and setting of the sun, is it you or is it me?

which one of us is visible and which one is veiled?
the hidden trap that silently awaits, is it you or is it me?

who has cast a shadow on the full moon's glorious face?
the cloud that threatens to block it out, is it you or is it me?

these homes have lost their colour because of the wind and rain
who lives in this deep silence of the town, is it you or is it me?

it feels like the houses and the doors are calling out, Muneer
the name that everyone has forgotten, is it you or is it me?

a strange flower has bloomed on the throne, it's the moonlit night's fault

a strange flower has bloomed on the throne, it's the moonlit night's fault
I felt like a hand had drawn a bow and shot an arrow to my heart

there must have been a reason that she promised and did not come
maybe the gathering storm scared her, maybe it was distrust

when my heart was afire, I didn't complain, I kept my dignity
no one else in this world could pull off this feat I achieved

up in the sky that red of the kite flying over there
is the flame of a lamp lit by a hennaed hand and floated in the air

my powers include a kind of magic, through many ages it has come to me
when I think of her I can call her, I can make her whatever I want her to be

the rose was there and the clouds and an elegant face

the rose was there and the clouds and an elegant face
but in my heart there was a longing for another face

I wish that someone could have seen the castles I built in the air
I lived in the wild but had a habit of building to pass the days

I somehow managed to confess the thing that had been bothering me
the credit goes to the strange weather partly, and partly to my bravery

I lived in unfamiliar towns all through my days
although all the ease of home was not so far away

I hardly ever think of them now, what a tragedy, Muneer
those companions of a bygone time who were once so dear to me

your being with me was needed, your leaving was needed too

your being with me was needed, your leaving was needed too
the memory of someone in my life, that was needed too

things cannot go on forever in the very same way
a break in continuity, that was needed too

on a rainy night my lover's home disappears from view
lightning lighting up that door, that was needed too

how long could I have thought of you on that difficult night?[6]
exhausted from the journey I slept, that was needed too

a variety of fruitless memories occupied my mind

a variety of fruitless memories occupied my mind
what conflicts did I get myself into, wasting so much time

it was like being under house arrest, the town where I stayed
the company of those townspeople felt like being in jail

if I were, my darling, then you and I would meet
I was a dream, I was unborn, I lived in people's grief

that flash of lightning lit the forest, the walls and the doors
for a moment every visible thing came to life in its glow

when death came, what did they want to say, at that final time?
what were they thinking, what thoughts came to my
 friends' minds?

their voices carried through the forest, Muneer, a very long way
those women's sorrows lived for a long time in the shivalays

I no longer feel like going to see her when it rains

I no longer feel like going to see her when it rains
let the koels sing, I don't have time to spare

my heart keeps telling me, why don't you keep her by your side?
but her sensual beauty costs money, I don't have money to pay

the people of this place must have embittered him
he has the heart of a poet, why would a poet hate?

perhaps I could have stopped it when it first began
now the town's madness has gone beyond what I can restrain

I am looking all around, perhaps it will appear
in the expanse of the forest, there is no human face

in this journey of dreams, Muneer, this must be another stage
I clearly don't belong here, in the misery of this stranger's place

the glory of art is nothing, the poet's poetry here is nothing

the glory of art is nothing, the poet's poetry here is nothing
the pride of the rich is nothing, the poor's modesty here
    is nothing

there is no foundation for anything in this town
even the value of Alexander here is nothing

no connection left to the ways of times gone by
there is nothing on the horizon either, there is nothing

the same night of separation, the same forest, the same place
there is no way to cross this river of sorrow, there is nothing

unattainability is the destiny of this town
nothing to be found outside, inside there is nothing

it’s not at all certain that she also thinks of me

it’s not at all certain that she also thinks of me
the way I feel about her is also the way she feels

a few more hearts should melt in this city made of stone
some more sorrow should be added to this sorrow-laden breeze

let’s talk a little so that our hearts can stay in touch
let’s dream a dream together of the day when we can meet

this reality we live in, this world that we can see
may exist only in the minds of the dead, or in one of
    their dreams

this destructible town swaggers because there’s water nearby
if there was no water here then where would this town be?

this world is an entity that is perishing as we speak
every single thing in it points to mortality

from some side it should come, some happy news, Muneer
by day or by night, miraculously

this earth, this whole world, is a secret unrevealed

this earth, this whole world, is a secret unrevealed
who lives in the present and the past is a secret unrevealed

these waters are a secret with their boundless expanse
this weighty dream of a mighty peak is a secret unrevealed

I occasionally unveil it in some lines of poetry
this world of thoughts of beauty is a secret unrevealed

the going and returning of the seasons is a mystery
like a tree in spring, the leaf in fall is a secret unrevealed

who does the whole world wait for impatiently?
who has been sent here is a secret unrevealed

my verses are obscure to them, Muneer
to me the language of this town is a secret unrevealed

creepers climbed the doors and walls slowly

creepers climbed the doors and walls slowly
voices faded from this town slowly

clouds appeared quietly over the withering gardens
the trees swayed in the cool breeze slowly

blood took its own time to show its colour
this mark turned a deep red slowly

gold's lustre brought it to these houses made of ash
the snake made its home in human bodies slowly

dust and ash and rain had made walls around me
the news of your grief reached me slowly

Muneer, has some evil spirit cast a shadow on this country?
we thrash around, frantic, but travel very slowly

weakness of body and soul gave birth to a kind of strength

weakness of body and soul gave birth to a kind of strength
this noise that fills the city was born from speechlessness

she nurtures fancies of living for a long time
this desire for excess came from the mortality of life

I didn't believe in anything, and that's why I failed
it could never trust, my heart is to blame

in this world with six sides, there could be some sign of me
this suspicion was planted in my head by my anonymity

Muneer, I've been on the wrong road from the very first day
I realized this when I realized that this journey was in vain

as soon as evening came that memory returned

as soon as evening came that memory returned
as soon as the lamps were lit, my heart flickered out

the doors of the city of sorrow fell open
as soon as a light breeze began to blow

who were you? I never saw you again
as soon as I rubbed my eyes, the dream disappeared

my own house fills me with fear
as soon as the luminous moon appears

it feels like something changes in you
as soon as your shadow on the wall changes

it's like blood has stained my hands
as soon as I crushed the flower, a poison ran through me

there is light and more light over there

there is light and more light over there
there is life and more life over there

the torments that we suffer over here
their opposite is found over there

a home that is like a heart's desire
a dream is played out over there

its pieces have scattered over here
beauty has one face over there

the one you wanted over here, Muneer
the joy of meeting her is over there

clouds in spring, this evening of longing is just a dream

clouds in spring, this evening of longing is just a dream
this waiting for my beautiful love is just a dream

these stories of meeting and parting are just a fantasy
the tale of her grief and my sorrow is just a dream

they're like a dream, those bygone times and those homes
the magical thought of tomorrow's happiness is just a dream

just a dream the house lit by the morning's light
the dream dreamt on a bitter night is just a dream

in this very town, Muneer, I meet her every day
but I know that beautiful idol is just a dream

I was the life of the party but I began to fade away

I was the life of the party but I began to fade away
what was I once, not long ago, and what am I today?

this unfamiliar age made me lonelier each day
slowly, inexorably, the world drifted away

the gates of the city of parting seemed to be lying in wait
just one knock and they started falling open, all the gates

words fell like curtains over what I wanted to say
it turned into 'without', every word in this place

time has passed so fast, Muneer, engaged in the everyday
today kept turning into tomorrow and the days just blew away

the mirror doesn't take me away any more

the mirror doesn't take me away any more
I am in prison, it doesn't let me go

the mighty mountain is unendingly stoic
written teachings don't make any noise

the gathering's mood changes constantly
the mood doesn't believe in fidelity

don't hanker after worldly pleasure
it's never found, this hidden treasure

you do whatever pleases yourself
you don't listen to anyone else

there is always a successor
no throne remains vacant forever

Muneer, it is coming, the age of justice
tyranny and oppression are never endless

it is not going to become a cry, the silence

it is not going to become a cry, the silence
the doors of prison are not going to open

in sorrow unbroken I always thought
the bonds of my sorrow are not going to loosen

I met that beautiful one as if
I am never going to part from her after meeting

I am worshipping those idols assiduously
who are never going to be our supreme being

Muneer this beautiful life that we live
cannot remain forever unchanging

shade keeps decreasing

shade keeps decreasing
forests keep receding

an unyielding prayer
that I keep repeating

look, the sun is about to break
the clouds are dissipating

all the sights around me
appear to be retreating

look, Muneer, the garden in spring
like colours are adhering

every moment every breath

every moment every breath
just the fear of dying

there is also happiness here
O my habit of grieving

is there someone over there?
O road to the realm of dying

in the light of the idols
the flags of grief are drooping

this is the truth, Muneer
you are dreaming

how do I reveal my grief?

how do I reveal my grief?
how do I make silence speak?

I want to refashion this earth
how do I do it, it's heaven's work?

I just can't bring myself to trust any man
how do I find a confidant?

I am thinking to myself on a dark night
how do I make the Milky Way appear in the sky?

I'm a bird of the forest, tell me, my heart
how do I make a nest among flowers?

Muneer, in these times of woe
how do I take care of body and soul?

so much of the night is gone and I have yet to sleep

so much of the night is gone and I have yet to sleep
in this town I have yet to dream a happy dream

why did you give your heart to that young one at such an age?
when something like a heart is just a toy for her to play

I am surrounded by such memories from which there is no gain
how much longer will I wander among them, how many
more days?

what happened, friends, was meant to be and so it came to pass
I have yet to wash this cruel age's stains off my heart

once again, I want to see the flower beds bloom in spring
the dirt that surrounds this town still has some gold within

let's go and sit at the feet of the much praised One, Muneer
and spend some time thinking about that which is yet to be

in the shadow of my beloved's mansion

in the shadow of my beloved's mansion
I sat in my intoxication

she came, but in a dream she came
and here I was sitting in wait

like her face there are no faces
look at her sitting with the masses

happiness fills her with fear
what delusion has made its home in her

I was also roaming the roads, Muneer
he was also sitting in the street

there are some other stories that I don't ever reveal

there are some other stories that I don't ever reveal
there are some other sorrows of which I never speak

I am the sole guardian of some secrets in this world
there is some news that I never share with anyone

everybody claims to have a talent that they lack
no one proudly displays what they are in fact

forbearance is my strength in the hardest of times
a man with this quality can be in sorrow but not cry

I too am in love with the beauties of this town, Muneer
but I don't believe in wasting my life on this fancy

the reality that I sought couldn't be found

the reality that I sought couldn't be found
I didn't find any friend in these towns

I continue to suspect that I exist in these times
I haven't been able to get this thought out of my mind

although I had wanted to be with her for a little while
but in these days and these nights, I couldn't find the time

I needed some time from her, I had something to say
but I didn't get that time, there was no time to spare

I had to leave her, Muneer, after a little while
that unfaithful one's disposition didn't quite match mine

the mystery of this unknown town faded a little

the mystery of this unknown town faded a little
in this journey my fervent madness faded a little

the beauty I had never seen, I saw it in front of me
the poverty of the morning and night of my life faded a little

things were hidden by a veil, it was the cause of my uncertainty
once we met face to face that unfamiliarity faded a little

it eased the sorrow of exile, promenading around the world
this way my heart's melancholy faded a little

I had to draw a boundary somewhere in the endless, Muneer
once I built a house my uneasiness faded a little

a world of exile is all that I liked

a world of exile is all that I liked
this desolate house is all that I liked

an anonymous life in a decrepit quarter
this town was charming then, a place that I liked

the rising sun had coloured everything red
I liked that face then, when I saw it in that light

my heart is quite happy that we have separated
a boundary line was never something I liked

the way she came to me, Muneer, without any fear
my heart liked that strange spectacle last night

if I live or if I die, what difference does it make?

if I live or if I die, what difference does it make?
if I make no sound and pass away, what difference does it make?

what does my existence amount to in this age?
I am a dream, if I scatter what difference does it make?

who remains waiting for me over there?
if I go home when evening comes, what difference does it make?

this pain will stay in my heart as long as I live
even if I cross the river of sorrow, what difference does it make?

who do I complain to and what do I say?

who do I complain to and what do I say?
if I emulate these pointless ways, what difference does it make?

the thing that is bound to perish eventually
if I protect it so assiduously, what difference does it make?

falsehood has come to rule in this town of God
if I speak the truth in these towns, what difference does it make?

Muneer, everything is meaningless in this place
if I submit or I revolt, what difference does it make?

is this a memory of a night from a year gone by?

is this a memory of a night from a year gone by?
the same breeze had blown in the garden, the same clock
had chimed

lying in the trunk its begun to smell strange
the handkerchief of silk has begun to fade

the fear of death filled the town on the moon's fourth day
these caves made of bricks were in terror of an earthquake

an evening crazed by colour was leaning over the sea
or it was the portrait of a thought within a dream

as the years add up people become strange
I felt sad today when I saw that beautiful one's state

he looked at me intently and then he fell silent
it still bothers me, that unasked question

it blew the cloak of modesty away

it blew the cloak of modesty away
the wind took the leaves of the garden away

the words that had made their home in my heart
when I called out, they travelled a very long way

I kept walking the long and difficult road
as long as the ultimate showed me the way

when the evening of the magic of fidelity went
it took the colour of the horizons away

there used to be an ancient sign on the shore
the current of the river washed it away

Muneer, there was such beauty in that age
some calamity came and took it away

how was I to account for the way that I lived?

how was I to account for the way that I lived?
the questions were all wrong, what answer could I give?

centuries of wretchedness had left me dreamless
what could dreams give in these vacuums without end?

like the breeze my lovers' hearts liked to roam
how could I torment them by giving them one home?

the confinement of law made my heart want inebriation
how could I give it drink in such constriction?

Muneer, the forest was like a mirage from the first
how could I give that mirror the lustre of my thirst?

there are a million worlds flourishing in my heart

there are a million worlds flourishing in my heart
ignore everyone and, some day, come stay in my heart

it descends quietly in the silence of the night
the Milky Way of your beauty, finds its way to my heart

waves of light rise from the roads
there are shadows that sob quietly in my heart

light rains down again on palace and street
again it feels like dusk in my heart

the world talks about what the world cares about
the story of my sorrow stays in my heart

why would one be in this destructible world?
stay, and stay eternal, stay in my heart

look into her eyes and see

look into her eyes and see
submit to this lie and see

what secret hides in separation
find out for yourself and see

in the silence of a lonely evening
sing yourself old songs and see

say to yourself: this night is dark
then light up some lamps and see

the heart is a desolate house
dance and sing sadness and see

you've spent your life waking all night
go to the doors of sleep and see

if this earth cannot provide refuge the sky is always there

if this earth cannot provide refuge the sky is always there
something to tell my heart, some tale is always there

the skin has turned sallow but the lips are still red
in the vastness of the desert's spread a garden is still there

an eagle sits atop a dome under a blazing sun
these streets have been ravaged but a guardian is still there

you may, in fact, find him, why not call out and see?
if not this fruitless journey of a lifetime is still there

you and I are very close, Muneer, nonetheless
between us something like a curtain is certainly there

these silent doors and thresholds alone

these silent doors and thresholds alone
these ravaged desolate homes alone

when I got up and left in my drunkenness
I don't know where I went heedless alone

a grim forest on all sides
the entire journey I walked alone

like a breeze blew through colour
she stood on the balcony alone

the pallid light of evening falls
like it's still daytime but the town is alone

Muneer, when I left home I too
wandered from door to door alone

on the night of meeting why did I dream of distance?

on the night of meeting why did I dream of distance?
at the zenith of victory why did the doors of fear open?

why did so many hearts fill with suspicions this year?
why did restlessness strike this town of patience ?

the flowers are lit by a strange fire this spring
why did an excess of flowers come this year in the garden?

if it was her then why this indifference on her face?
it was such a short sojourn, why this revolution?

just a carnival of greed in every direction
why did my heart's cry run into this illusion?

I am not happy at being so far away from her
when I wasn't there, why did her beauty ripen?

lightning blazes on the parapet made of cloud
why did this storm come like a great affliction?

why did you lose faith in her, Muneer?
why are you tormented by suspicion?

I'll go now and see what state it's in, that path

I'll go now and see what state it's in, that path
many years have gone by since I saw it last

the waking dream will return from its journey to this very place
eagerly, fearfully, people will watch from windows and doorways

other people also live here, it's not a desert, it's a town
when has he been aware enough to notice houses all around

he has to go and you have to go too, there is nothing left to say
then why delay him without reason, why not let him go his way?

go to the garden, O sweet one, it's come, the breeze of spring
it's a pale breeze in a strange forest, a strange magic rules over it

every page is a golden door, Muneer, these ghazals of yours
when you finish writing this book, go and show it to her

when evening came the desolate tavern's door fell open

when evening came the desolate tavern's door fell open
in my dream the gate to past companionships fell open

the fidelity of this age was just a frenzied dream
a whole lifetime passed before this old secret opened

a thrill ran through the forest when the cloud and breeze came
like an army of trees felt their chains of sorrow open

she began to glow in the dark whenever I would stir
my eyes lighted on that idol's mysterious talent

the smell of new shoots along the river's bank, Muneer
the colour of the clouds above like an umbrella opened

I have to cross the desolation of a desert of voices calling out

I have to cross the desolation of a desert of voices calling out
one journey is completed another one is yet to start

these doors appear as if entangled by the fallen walls
the cold wind baulks in fear at their dusty thresholds

the terror of loneliness will suffuse desert and mountain with fear
at midnight, cutting through the darkness, when the moon appears

it's like it has just begun, the wonder is still obscure
the eye is going to become finer, the colour will mature

like a streak of blood descends into the yellowness of gold
the violent intoxication of the poison of gold will descend into the soul

how many stages of the journey remain?

how many stages of the journey remain?
in this body how much life remains

in the homes of living people
the habits of dead people remain

meeting her in that dream life
the dream is gone, desires remain

the springs of colour and light have flowed away only
their colour still remains
I owe my existence to them, my heart! in this town those
faces remain

Muneer, she came and has gone too
something like a fragrance in this garden remains

the frightened people trusted someone, who was it?

the frightened people trusted someone, who was it?
who did I wait for all my life long, who was it?

the street was empty when the dust blew through it
what person was in that dust, whose dust was it?

you dragged me through the world from door to door
who were you thinking of, restless heart, who was it?

near that house, so unusually built
whose garland was that, whose blood was it?

Muneer, life is nothing but a continuous threat of death
who in the world ever had any control on it?

perfection knows no boundaries

perfection knows no boundaries
there is no limit to beauty

near or far, those same destinations
that same evening of dreams and ruminations

nor do I know where she is
nor does she know what state I am in

is this the answer to my call?
or her question called out in response?

this is the time of evening prayer
the day begins its decline here

those calamities that happened here
were held in trust for many years

there is something in your eyes, Muneer
some kind of sorrow very deep

another chapter of the book of life is over

another chapter of the book of life is over
beauty is over, one kind of strife is over

the journey is free now of the desert's deception
the mirages are gone, the restlessness is over

the cloud poured and then opened out into the night's breeze
the lightning's angry confusion is over

the mountain and desert offer repose, the evening is calm
the dream of a world of difficulty and sorrow is over

I am no longer answerable to anyone, Muneer
that one question and its answer are over

the tired sun set, the garden of stars glowed

the tired sun set, the garden of stars glowed
at the summits of the trees like a lamp the moon glowed

the flame of days gone by made my mind glow
'lost happinesses lie this way', a sign began to glow

every street begins to fill with henna's perfume
in this flowing fragrance every heart's flame glowed

a red river of wine has begun to flow
the ruby goblet of a wanton's blood has begun to glow

the magic of your hand that we saw

the magic of your hand that we saw
people still talk about what we saw

the girls fill with joy when clouds fill the sky
monsoon flowers bloom on rooftops at the sight

my heartache took me to the location
where the doors of enchantment lay open

when the breeze blew, they rose as one all aflutter
the birds that had made their home in old quarters

you exist in no place, in no place is there me
these are all figments of a reverie

Muneer, here is the moment of meeting at last
the night of separation is long in the past

what am I without you, come out now and see

what am I without you, come out now and see
if you have the courage, look into my eyes and see

the evening is dark, the wind is blowing, night is about to fall
the traveller who passed by, light his lamp and see

the sound of footsteps outside the door approaches and then recedes
who is in the empty street, call him near and see

it could be that someone will look and be amazed
on the walls of your room, draw something and see

you too need to learn to live with others now in this world, Muneer
you've seen it from the outside, now go inside and see

the colourful cloaks were coloured strange colours

the colourful cloaks were coloured strange colours
it felt like my heart and my life were gripped by terrors

enchantment on their lips, eyes filled with grief
they wore new jewellery on their feet

somewhere it was the scent of your clothes
like the night's breeze was carrying a garden afloat

when I looked around after taking a few sips
I saw a vacuum with people and houses floating in it

they wander today on the streets, these flames
they used to live in dark mountain caves

he might not have left if I had stopped him
but I was caught up in my own whims

Muneer, it was like a box of colours had opened
the air was filled with those kinds of visions

those who forget me, I too will forget them

those who forget me, I too will forget them
I'll grind it into dust, their arrogance

I see all their faces, I hear what they say
I'll settle all of their accounts one day

I will show how to light up these benighted towns
I will start up a luminous breeze all around

villages without compare, gardens without boundaries
my dreams will show within people's dreams

Muneer, I'll go one day, I'll go to her house
I'll stand at her door, I'll stand and call out

the happy morning, the night's grief

the happy morning, the night's grief
was it a fable or was it reality?

neither did I meet her, nor did I talk to her
our relationship was wrapped in mystery

the manner I had adopted
was an excuse for us to meet

over there was a memory great and noble
and there was this age in between

Muneer, I too came into being
it was just a formality

my heart in a state of ease I saw

my heart in a state of ease I saw
in the spring this wondrous scene I saw

whoever I loved I loved in intoxication
whoever I saw in dust I saw

giving great importance to desires
this quality in my friend I saw

I saw one person in many people
in the confines of entirety I saw

whenever I saw this earth, Muneer
it was imprisoned in night and day I saw

the stories of separation turned unreal by and by

the stories of separation turned unreal by and by
this earth began to feel like a mirage in the sky

which bad sign was the beauty of this life born under?
in which false home did the truth get wasted by and by?

the constrictions of today carry indications of what is to come
a stubbornness became the mark of happiness by and by

the one who knew the other side didn't say a word
and so that story kept being told only from one side

Muneer, a whole world was created by just one cry
the single fragrant bud became the whole garden by and by

a dream journey seems to rob my legs of life

a dream journey seems to rob my legs of life
an unending hard journey in pallid moonlight

strong is the stench of the buds of death by an unseen hand
like water closing in around the dryness of the land

the fruit of continuous toil is an unending dejection
I work in the air, I seek a rare perfection

it troubles me in my house, the urge to roam in the vast
the sky never stops affecting the arch in my backyard

silences, and so extreme, whatever happened, O Muneer?
wherever did it acquire such a trait, this mercury?

the threat to this journey from its start, is it that calamity?

the threat to this journey from its start, is it that calamity?
or is it just the breeze? open the door and see

the eye of the mirror is known but not the image within
what if the very thing that's seen is actually hidden?

water all around it, water underneath
maybe it is floating, this town that seems firm on its feet

the desert of death may lie that way, beyond that point don't go
if you want to turn back, you find there is no road

I don't return home because this thought prevents my return
perhaps the sight of me will upset that beautiful one

all your life, Muneer, thoughts of her consumed you
the real fun of it is that she didn't have a clue

apart from the moonlight that provokes frenzies

apart from the moonlight that provokes frenzies
there is nothing left in the town apart from the breeze

there is another face somewhere that is just like mine
there is another place somewhere apart from the village of cries

there is another road I can take so that she and I can meet
there are other marks apart from the prints of her feet

Kufa is in decline, beggars walk the streets
there is no gate open apart from the gate of the plea

the limits of earth and sky, houses of gold, lips that speak
you can see everything here apart from the Supreme Being

my desires are the cause of my sorrow, Muneer
nothing torments me apart from the phrase 'I need'

in this mortal world I have been through many tests

in this mortal world I have been through many tests
I've had to bear many sorrows in my state of homelessness

there is at least its likeness, a dream of an eternal spring
the image is overflowing with the smell of the real thing

this sleeping and this waking in the coming and going
    of night and day
in these symbols those who think can find many places to stay

many koels sang there, near the wall of the garden
the clear water of the tank glittered with the moon's effulgence

what memories it had, where it left them, it doesn't care
    to know
the heart is a rapid river with a breakneck flow

I saw you speaking today in that gathering, Muneer
you who were famous for the fact that you didn't speak

injustice goes a long way in less inhabited towns

injustice goes a long way in less inhabited towns
fidelity goes a long way in less inhabited towns

spring stays for long in villages with few people
autumn goes a long way in less inhabited towns

laughter or concern or the sound of someone sighing
voices carry a long way in less inhabited towns

when the night is dark, the lamp on the empty road
casts its light a long way in less inhabited towns

in the manner of the people of populated towns, Muneer
the breeze travels a long way in less inhabited towns

all night long I stayed awake in grief

all night long I stayed awake in grief
in the morning in the garden I was sleeping a deep sleep

a seven-coloured garland was lying next to me
somehow, I had reached an unknown city

a new age came and brought order to my life
the enchantment of another age had completely scattered me

these parts looked familiar when evening began to fall
I've travelled these roads before, the thought occurred to me

I got scared when my sorrowing friend knocked
some tragedies of the age had struck terror into me

I myself got lost, Muneer, in a wish that had no name
it was in search of something that I had come out into the street

if she appears before you, don't look at her

if she appears before you, don't look at her
even if she leaves you, don't think of her

forget the one who's gone, once she's gone away
it's like a lost thought, don't give it life again

his words are now empty of all meaning, Muneer
don't stop him, whatever he says, just let him speak

a crude way of thinking had enchanted me

a crude way of thinking had enchanted me
I was kept apart from the world by my own conceit

there was no good reason to break journey over there
but I was rendered helpless by my own fatigue

she looked at me for a long time but she did not speak
I was distressed for a long time by that memory

the darkness was intense in those parts, Muneer
but the sorcery of grief made a torch out of me

it burst and poured down, the dark cloud of resentment

it burst and poured down, the dark cloud of resentment
when I nudged him last night my friend began to open

beautiful people came out in the streets as soon as evening fell
on every road the perfumers brought out their wares to sell

I tried very hard but couldn't keep it out of sight
as a result, the secret of my sorrowing heart came to light

closed in the intoxications of the night's festivities
the shining eyes opened when they felt the morning breeze

Muneer, when she came out on the roof up above
it seemed like in the sky a marketplace of colour had
    opened up

don’t fall so silent

don’t fall so silent
don’t grieve like this in parting

dreams are for dreaming
don’t make them your dwelling

your complaint will not be heeded
don’t complain to a tyrant

they may give birth to stories
don’t write words and erase them

some consideration for your status, Muneer
don’t make everyone your friend

let the rays of the brilliant sun be born from the nights

let the rays of the brilliant sun be born from the nights
let grief give birth to the dream of delight

the one who has disappeared should appear once more
from complication should emerge the way to the city of the pure

flower of hope! bloom in the wilderness of futility
from the camel's saddle should come the picture of fidelity[7]

come from the direction I least expect
be born in a place I don't know exists

let throngs of the dead manifest the breath of the living
O true intent, be born from the worst of cravings

like a rainbow emerge after the rain
let the beauty of colour be heightened by the open plains

Muneer, let the Prophet's name light up the cities
let new homes give birth to an ancient dream

they went to green branch cities

they went to green branch cities
the birds of the wind went to the trees

a golden demon haunts that home
those who live there have taken to the road

those footprints in this impenetrable fog
god knows which way they wandered off

it was like just now there was someone right next to me
what strange suspicions came with the morning's dreams

in the lightning many colours were born
many shapes formed on the walls and the doors

on every side of me, that beauty that drives men insane
every face seems to remind me of that face

why this great sadness today, Muneer?
what were those shadows that passed over land and sea?

a story out of order is what it looked to be

a story out of order is what it looked to be
was it some kind of spectacle or a madman's dream?

the characters were connected in a disconnected way
their unconsciousness was filled with a kind of regret
    at being aware

when I fell in love in my time of waywardness
it was just a way of calming my heart's restlessness

I really want to leave my house and travel a long way
but my heart's greatest desire was to come back home always

when I took my heart into that gathering, Muneer
that beauty decided to act coy in the assembly

again the morning breeze fills the heart with grief

again the morning breeze fills the heart with grief
the thought of the one I lost again returns to me

it was strange to remember that old home at this age
in the years when, from homes, it's time to prepare to leave

they would have made a fine example if they were still here
but I took those goodnesses and dumped them in the stream

the answers to which were probably not to be found at
my destination
along the way I was assailed by such questions

if it hadn't been, Muneer, that today was just like yesterday
the work I put off till tomorrow, I would have done today

this is what I do, my friends, spill my heart's blood all the time

this is what I do, my friends, spill my heart's blood all the time
lighting the lamp of poetry while staying up late into
these nights

you wayward ones who wander in forests far from home
now and then, when time permits, go and visit your homes

scattered and forgotten memories bloom like flowers in the
wilderness of night
take the strong alcohol of sorrow and try to erase their
sharp outlines

what multifarious colours are painted behind this fragrant wall
before the day's sun rises find out about them all

now you too, Muneer, keep some distance between those
streets and yourself
from dishonest lying people it's better to protect yourself

the night's inkiness has faded

the night's inkiness has faded
the night has become more obfuscated

it carries all my dreams away
this season has become the season to migrate

shot through with the primeval morning's grief
the breeze feels like an early morning's breeze

it's like it has learned the whole secret
life has become a 'no' endlessly repeated

Muneer, it ends in a distress with no use
the torment of migration has reduced

a garden of lightning in the clouds, I could have shown it to her

a garden of lightning in the clouds, I could have shown it to her
I wish I had gone that night and woken her

the lost breeze wanders aimlessly around the thrones
I should have told it where the people who lived here have gone

that one who used to come and stand near you without a word
all she wanted was for you to call out to her

what you needed was sympathy, to call this love is not right
when your heart began to ache, you should have kept it
out of sight

what's the use even if I am to get her now, Muneer
it's taken my whole life to bring her around to me

it brightened up the courtyard, bathed all the vines

it brightened up the courtyard, bathed all the vines
it made the sky even bluer, the rain that came last night

in the sunlight pale flowers cover trees on every side
the streets are coloured yellow by a poisonous light

the pain his heart has borne was involved in it too
and partly it was intoxication that made him sing in tune

I sat down and have written out an account of heartache
a single drop of blood has coloured the whole page

the moon has risen over the village, look, see the light

the moon has risen over the village, look, see the light
it has coloured the houses, see, they were dark as night

your eyes deceive you in whatever that you see
always know that all these places are just a dream

pass through this world like you're on an excursion
think of it as a long period of separation

if the shadow of gold falls on him, he begins to brighten up
look at him, in his unconscious state, Adam made from dust

in this place when clouds gather, they fill me with fear
this is a city of locked doors, see the number of walls here

a heavy shadow falls on them of forgotten memories
when evening falls see how the beautiful ones go into frenzies

its absence has left many hearts with a scar that still won't fade
the truth is that, like the morning breeze, the flower
just flew away

if someone calls you from behind in the jungles, Muneer
don't ever turn around, don't turn around to see

it feels like this town is near here somewhere

it feels like this town is near here somewhere
in this dust there is the gleam of gold here and there

at the other end of the garden there is a thicket of
trees untamed
but you would never know it if you looked at the arch of
the gate

on the banks a storm with clouds and wind is hiding
the stream, meanwhile, appears to drown you in silence

in this age a futile death is the reward for those who care
every moment a sense of loss floats in the air

a clean sheet covers the land of cacophony
like a strange bedcover at a mortuary

Muneer, this rose-like redness you see in my eyes
is the colour of the thorns of spring sticking in my side

my lover's beauty is hard to put into words

my lover's beauty is hard to put into words
I try but I find there's no end to this work

every ruin is not attractive
every old house is not Jamshed's palace

spend a whole life watching the road the dead went
I don't think any gaze has such endurance

this is my punishment now that I am by myself
my head doesn't even bow to you, it never did to anyone else

my heart is so numb, Muneer, from continuous defeat
even if someone leaves, I don't feel any grief

there is a mark against my name

there is a mark against my name
a shadow over all I say

is this a mountain in front of me
or a book placed conspicuously

waiting for a gaze that sees
some light waits on a balcony

a flock of birds is this city
fallen on net and seeds

my own sorrow, I sometimes kept in me
sometimes I wept at the world's grief

Muneer, I am constantly amazed
I am standing at such a place

a singular idea and dreams so many

a singular idea and dreams so many
a question alone, answers so many

they never spared a thought for their own worth
so many were ruined in this world, so many

I too had to give an account of myself
I who was without limit

a thousand things said in one gaze
and after that there were so many veils

like the colour red turned fragrant
so many roses bloomed, so many

Muneer, how did they appear in my heart
so many new anxieties, so many?

wounded by the sword of its own glamour

wounded by the sword of its own glamour
the moon lost its mind when it looked into the water

such a strong wind picked up, by evening the streets
were deserted
such heavy rain fell, the whole town was flooded

the evening was ablaze with colour, when I journeyed alone
then, even from my eyes, this beautiful sight was gone

where will he be, and, wherever he is, will he be the same now?
and this thought, when it came, further weighed my heart down

Muneer, on the night of meeting, beauty filled me with terror
it was like my hand went limp with an excess of desire

the time to leave is here, in what worlds should I live?

the time to leave is here, in what worlds should I live?
which regions should I settle in, in what houses should I live?

on every side of me is a wilderness with no homes
when I leave this wilderness, in what places should I live?

where should I divulge this knowledge that I have?
or till eternity should I stay where this secret's custodians live?

the dark night of separation, and beyond it human settlements
the same dream eternally, in whichever age I might live

this journey is from the known to the known, Muneer
in the prison of these boundaries, how can I live?

in the intoxication of night, I offered her my salute

in the intoxication of night, I offered her my salute
I ended up doing what I wanted to do

she came in a pale cloak to the gathering and sat
she held a flower of henna in her hand

I had managed to keep our love concealed
she revealed the heart's secret in her simplicity

when I woke, the road was in a state of desolation
it was evening now and I had to reach my destination

Muneer, the weariness of travel had made my body lifeless
in the middle of the journey, it was a bad idea to rest

the glint of the sun, the lightning flash, in the spring I have seen the green forest

the glint of the sun, the lightning flash, in the spring I have
seen the green forest
filled with the rustling of colourful soft leaves, I have seen
such a forest

the wall of the sky, the archway of time, these are all illusions
that pass
this one truth has come along with me, since I saw the
blooming forest

this world inherits a covenant of a life to be lived in some dream
a story of Adam alone who has seen the lonely forest

a gateway for the breeze, a green cloak, a secret from a
thousand years ago
changing colour all the time, each moment I have seen a
new forest

I saw him in that house, Muneer, but it felt like this to me
by the banks of a river, surrounded by water, as if I was
seeing a forest

I am hearing the inaudible

I am hearing the inaudible
I am seeing the invisible

I really want to rest, to break journey
the enchantment of this night of devastation doesn't set me free

beauty wants to embellish the gathering
but its strength is robbed by the grief of its first unveiling

it was like the scene was being set for earth and sky to meet
it became so dark that it was impossible to see

go on, throw open the doors to the land of prayer, Muneer
why are you silent? why don't you cry out and plead?

I am so tired I am finding it difficult to walk along the way

I am so tired I am finding it difficult to walk along the way
it was I who was at the height of my powers, and it is
I who am in decline today

walking down the road, I keep stopping to look
I have a feeling you are around here somewhere

this spectacle around me will last till my eyes open
I am dreaming but I am also aware

its enjoyment makes me fear death
the fear of that same thing makes life a travail

this darkness of the evening of travel, Muneer, feels a little burnt
along with happiness, I feel a sadness that is strange

wherever the feet go, a fear walks along with them

wherever the feet go, a fear walks along with them
wherever desert wanderers go, the desert goes along with them

hands have a strange connection with the hidden word
when secrets are spoken hands shake along with them

a wall of lamentations rises on the outskirts of the town
ancient homes and the quiet of the streets with them

the sun's glare is like poison for the beauty of colour
the gardens have something like a fever upon them

the moon reveals itself on a night of cloud and rain
like dark caves have a white light shining within

I have come here for some reason, Muneer
my dreams admit this thought, this idea stays with them

it took a meeting with strangers for her to lose her timidity

it took a meeting with strangers for her to lose her timidity
at least that playful one became a little more worldly

the sight of falling houses filled me with happiness
at least this town's heart was torn by the fear of itself

and now it happens that the moon is within man's reach
whatever it is, he has come to know the heavens at least

whatever she may or may not have felt on seeing me
the memory of the spring of beauty did fill her with grief

I must admit the struggle tired me out, Muneer
at least God's city was cleansed of tyranny

names without number and no sign to be seen

names without number and no sign to be seen
settlements upon settlements and not one sentry

cheerful and happy faces, hearts constant in orbit
there was such a land with no sky above it

what an evening it was, suspended between mornings
  and nights
and I was in those places where there was no one else in sight

every house was a secret because of those who lived in it
those people with whom I didn't share any relationship

someone was there on the other side of the walls
but there was a silence like there was no one at all

the flute sang out from all four directions, Muneer
but no one knew the secret of its cry in the city

there the sun climbs in the sky, here I wake from sleep

there the sun climbs in the sky, here I wake from sleep
along with me awakes all the beauty of the East

if I had not met her on this evening from the beginning of time
how would that dream of those walls and doors wake in this
heart of mine?

that charming one's waking is like the morning breeze
in the garden
as if behind the colours a colour wakes in the distance

that house no longer exists, but from that building if only
the city of my longings came into being before me

to see the moon rise above the endless sea, Muneer
and then, drawn by its allure, to see the waking sea

like a frightened snake that hides in a treasure chest

like a frightened snake that hides in a treasure chest
gold keeps everyone alive in this wilderness of dust

among the people of the town it's like performing a rite
travelling far from home each morning, coming back each night

eyes drenched in blue looked out upon the green
it was a reflection of the sky in the goblet maybe

buried underground the terror of cries that are voiceless
in a hidden dungeon something like lightning flashes

the brilliant evening of the town robbed more cheer
    from my heart
how much light has been wasted in lighting words of glass

I saw myself in the mirror, Muneer, and I was amazed
in some bygone time this used to be a different kind of face

in front of a million genealogies I stand alone

in front of a million genealogies I stand alone
like a soundless cry standing in front of domes

in the coming and going of breath, the outlines
    continuously blur
like voiceless lips opening in front of mirrors

breeze over the water and an unfamiliar land
dust swirls around in front of ancient banks

fire burns in homes or is it a picture
that stays in front of men as a reminder of Adam's misdemeanour?

enmity is the way of the world, an incorrect word is friendship
man stands alone in front of tyrants

there are four quiet things: land and water, sky and mountains
the heart trembles with fear in their desolate presence

Muneer, it's full of mystery, the wealthy man's mind
like the terror of a torchlit underground gold mine

my heart is in a strange quandary, what is the right direction?

my heart is in a strange quandary, what is the right direction?
memory pulls me backwards, hope in the forward direction

the one we had left to go to the wilderness of poverty
looking morning and evening in that home's shadow's direction

the day has just begun in this prison-like land
already all thoughts are drawn to the night guard's direction

a bright ray of morning light fell on the window
a face shone in the breeze in that glass's direction

both the destinations entice me from a distance, Muneer
in my dream I am travelling in a non-existent village's direction

last night multicoloured balls of fire lit up the firmament

last night multicoloured balls of fire lit up the firmament
then it rained so hard that the flowers and plants turned fragrant

every story of the magic in her eyes is true
all the tales of my heart bleeding are untrue

at first I felt ill at ease amongst the people of this foreign land
but slowly I lost all connections to my own homeland

all of them had come together and encouraged me, it is true
all my friends enjoyed the spectacle of my disgrace too

Muneer, when I passed by the window of a room
from between the slats of its blinds, silken buds were
    bursting through

it's like an old burden has gone and it's happy to be free

it's like an old burden has gone and it's happy to be free
the earth had grown dark because of an excess of trees

there is madness in the town at the sight of the new moon
the signs of evening falling have coloured all the views

it's hard like a stone, the heart of the ailing narcissus
the fever in its eyes is the torment of being beauteous

in the emptiness of mountain, forest and sea, that cry of mine
words fight each other in fear, imprisoned in that cry

an archway of sky between roof and door
a single lamp's flame seen through the window in the wall

I left her just because of something that I thought to myself
what a conclusion I drew from my lover's silence

the brilliance of the sun, Muneer, is in this body of mine
the night's eye is awestruck by my wandering light

after a while I began to think of her with antipathy

after a while I began to think of her with antipathy
and this brought a new kind of happiness to me

explaining dreams of frenzy is a difficult task
don't ask how much torment it has brought to me

we are separated by our different pedigrees
myself and the idols who nowadays fascinate me

for a hundred generations, my ancestors have been mercenaries
I achieved honour by way of poetry

there is someone, after all, who cares for me, Muneer
when I learned this, a strange astonishment filled me

Notes

1. The primary source of biographical information in the biographical sketch is *Muneer Niazi: Shakhs aur Shaer* (Misaal Publishers, Faislabad, 2014) by Dr Sumaira Ijaz. A portion of this work was made available by Dr Mohammad Mashhoor Ahmad. Dr Ijaz claims, on the basis of school records, that Muneer Niazi was born in 1922 although his year of birth is widely reported as 1928 on the Internet.
2. Muneer Niazi's unpublished interview quoted in *Muneer Niazi: Shakhs aur Shaer*, Misaal Publishers, Faislabad, 2014, by Dr Sumaira Ijaz.
3. Intizar Husain, ed. Farooq Argali, *Intekhab-e-Kulliyaat-e-Muneer Niazi* (Farid Book Depot, 2004).
4. 'Qisas al-Anbiya', Wikipedia, https://en.wikipedia.org/wiki/Qisas_Al-Anbiya.
5. After Laila and Majnun meet in the desert of Najd, Laila's mother carries her away on a camel while both were asleep. When Majnun wakes, he runs around the desert frantically searching for her.
6. The Urdu version refers to 'shaam-e-ghareeban', the night of Ashura after the martyrdom of Imam Hussain.
7. A reference to the story of Laila and Majnun.

Acknowledgements

First and foremost, thanks are due to Mrs Naheed Muneer Niazi who was very supportive of this effort. Without Sundeep Dougal and Omar Ali, who led me to Saeed Ahmed, the difficult process of securing the rights for this translation would have remained stalled. Major thanks are due to Saeed Sahib who actually secured the translation rights. Amitabh Chaudhary, Tanu Malik, Kishwar Khan, and Ahmed Kamal Rana also played vital roles in the process. Keshava Guha who was formerly at Juggernaut and Hoori Noorani at Liberty Books put in a lot of effort as well. Dr Mohammad Mashhoor Ahmad helped immensely by providing me access to authoritative biographical information on Muneer Niazi. Dr Farooq Argali's support was invaluable. On a personal note, I would like to thank Mohammad Noorul Islam who initiated my journey in Urdu poetry twenty-five years ago. Finally, I would like to thank my wife Ratika Kapur whose literary instincts I greatly rely on.

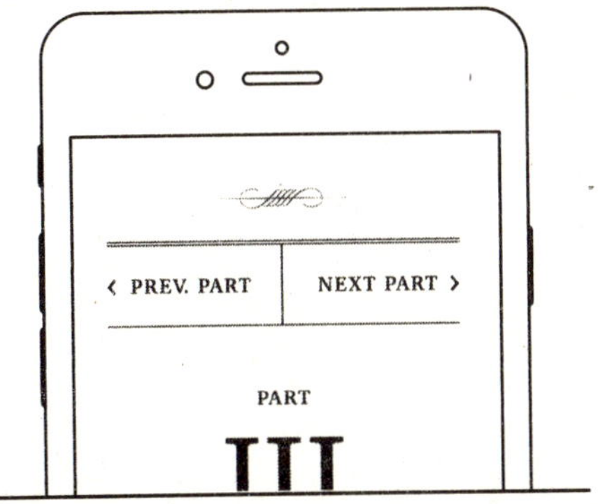

Beautiful Typography

The quality of print transferred to your mobile. Forget ugly PDFs.

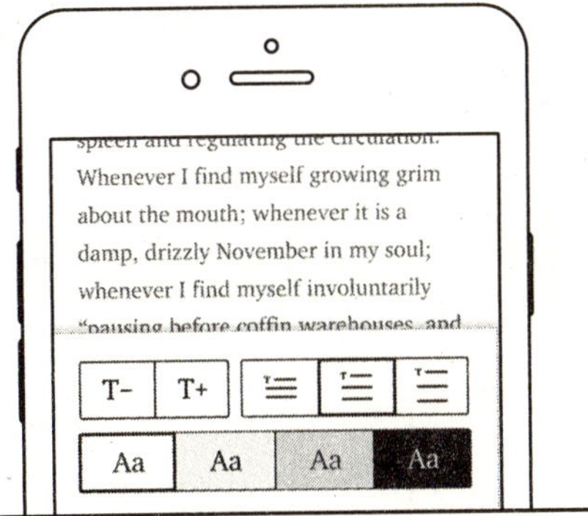

Customizable Reading

Read in the font size, spacing and background of your liking.

AN EXTENSIVE LIBRARY

Including fresh, new, original Juggernaut books from the likes of Sunny Leone, Praveen Swami, Husain Haqqani, Umera Ahmed, Rujuta Diwekar and lots more. Plus, books from partner publishers and loads of free classics. Whichever genre you like, there's a book waiting for you.

CRUCIBLES OF SIN
HITESHA
Can a Geek ever find Love?
Finding Juliet
Toffee
Mary Shelley
Frankenstein
A FAROOQ RESHI INVESTIGATION
COLD FLAKE
PRAVEEN SWAMI
A Psychiatrist's Guide To Heartbreak
How to Heal Your Broken Heart
DR SHYAM BHAT
MOIN and THE MONSTER
ANUSHKA RAVISHANKAR
stories of women from the ganglands
S. Hussain Zaidi with Jane Borges
Foreword by Vishal Bharadwaj
Pakistan's Queen of Romance
UMERA AHMED
Nowhere Girl
A Story of Love & Forgiveness
THE BEHEADING
This Is How He Will Bless Her
ABHEEK BARUA
THE Peshwa
The Lion and the Stallion
THE INVISIBLE WOMAN
SAURBH KATYAL
ANGRY BIRDS FAN? READ THE BOOK!
ANGRY BIRDS TOONS
TOONS TALES
ARCHANA SABOO
ADIKOOL
in #AfricanAdventures
i am not a bimbette
Tarana Khan
She hates me, He loves me not but...
DON'T FALL IN LOVE
Vandana Shankar
KHUSHWANT SINGH
WE INDIANS

Ask authors questions

Get all your answers from the horse's mouth. Juggernaut authors actually reply to every question they can.

Rate and review

Let everyone know of your favourite reads or critique the finer points of a book – you will be heard in a community of like-minded readers.

Gift books to friends

For a book-lover, there's no nicer gift than a book personally picked. You can even do it anonymously if you like.

Enjoy new book formats

Discover serials released in parts over time, picture books including comics, and story-bundles at discounted rates. And coming soon, audiobooks.

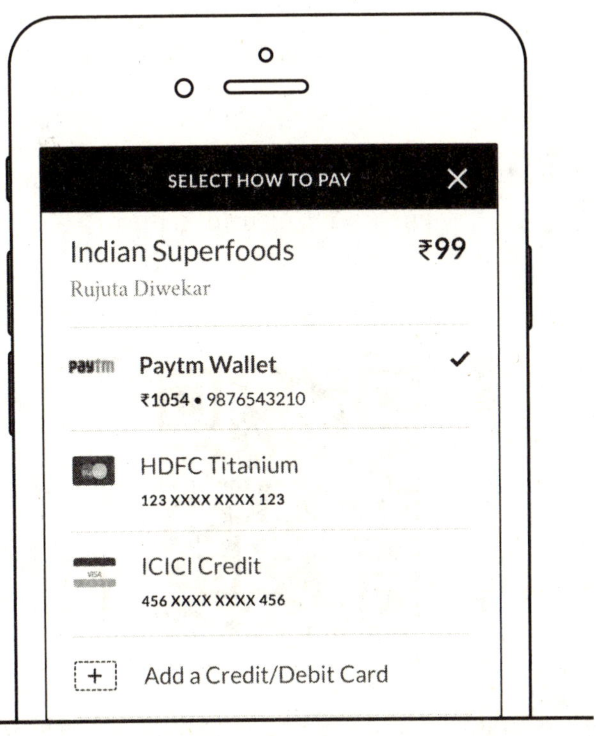

Paytm Wallet, Cards & Apple Payments

On Android, just add a Paytm Wallet once and buy any book with one tap. On iOS, pay with one tap with your iTunes-linked debit/credit card.

To download the app scan the QR Code
with a QR scanner app

For our complete catalogue, visit www.juggernaut.in
To submit your book, send a synopsis and two
sample chapters to books@juggernaut.in
For all other queries, write to contact@juggernaut.in